Thomas Hervey

A Letter from a Patriot in Retirement

to the right honourable Mr. William Pitt, upon the resigning of his

employment

Thomas Hervey

A Letter from a Patriot in Retirement
to the right honourable Mr. William Pitt, upon the resigning of his employment

ISBN/EAN: 9783337195847

Printed in Europe, USA, Canada, Australia, Japan

Cover: Foto ©ninafisch / pixelio.de

More available books at **www.hansebooks.com**

A
LETTER
FROM A
PATRIOT in RETIREMENT,

To the Right Honourable

Mr. WILLIAM PITT,

Upon the Refigning of his Employment.

Hoc caverat mens provida Reguli,
Diffentientis conditionibus
Foedis, et exemplo trahenti
Perniciem veniens in Ævum.
                    Hor. Lib. III. Od. 5.

" *Fear, admitted into public Counfels,*
" *Betrays like Treafon.*"
                    Addifon's Cato.

LONDON:

Printed for G. Woodfall, the Corner of Craig's
Court, Charing-Crofs. 1761.

(Price One Shilling and Six-Pence.)

Bookseller to the Reader.

I am order'd to inform the Public, that great part of this pamphlet was in the press a month ago : but the finishing and publication of it ha e been retarded, by a very disagreable accident, that intermediately happen'd in the author's family.

S I R,

THOUGH the news-writers, to the great reproach of the government, pretend to tell us what paffes in the cabinet, as confidently and familiarly as if they were members of it; I defire to avail myfelf no farther of public rumour, than is neceffary to make appofite, the *Latin* motto I have prefixed to this trifling lucubration. And if, as we are informed, the fchifm in his Majefty's counfels, has been created by a continuance of that fpirit in your's, to which we ftand indebted for the many advantages we have gained over our enemies; the propriety of the quotation, and your right to be fur-

named

named the *Englifh Regulus*, become equally unqueftionable.

The defcription I have taken the liberty to give of myfelf as a patriot, in this addrefs to you, is as little fictitious, as any thing elfe you will find there. I am a moft unfeigned friend to my country; and have afferted my claim to that character, in the prefent inftance, as a collateral proof of my being your's. For to love my country, and not to love you, who have been the greateft benefactor to it ever yet known, would be a kind of paradox. Your defire to be a man of bufinefs, and, when occafion offer'd, of fignalizing yourfelf in the fervice of the public, fhewed itfelf, from your very youth, to be a ruling inclination in you. Accordingly, you applied

plied yourſelf to the buſineſs of parliament, as ſoon as ever you had got a ſeat
there : wiſely foreſeeing, that a thorough
knowledge of thoſe matters could not fail
to prove a corner-ſtone to your noble ambition. Your progreſs in it was rapid,
and your diligence, which made it ſo, in-
defatigable. But a thorough diſapproba-
tion, at that time, both of men and mea-
ſures, and your bold avowal of it, was,
for many years, ſuch a check to your pur-
ſuit, that a leſs determined ſpirit, would
have hardly kept ſight of its illuſtrious object: by which is meant, ſome future poſ-
feſſion of a power in this country, obtained with honour, and ſupported with
abilities. Yet, on the other hand, the
ſtedfaſt oppoſition you gave to them,
ſhewed, that you was not only endued

B 2 with

with the unfafhionable virtue of felf-denial; but even capable of fuffering (to ufe a fcripture phrafe) for righteoufnefs fake. Your commiffion, when you had little elfe to live upon, became a forfeit to your inflexibility.————

As every thing that bears your name, at this time, will be fufficient to excite the curiofity of the public; it is to be pre-fumed, that I fhall have fome readers be-fide yourfelf. For which reafon, I thought it proper, to give this fhort account of your conduct, upon your firft outfet in life; in order to their better judging, whether you have been guilty of any deviations from your priftine doctrines, tenets, or purpofes, in the fubfequent parts of it. And what appearances foever there may

be

be againſt you, the preſumptions at leaſt in your favour will remain too ſtrong to be eaſily got over, by a diſpaſſionate and candid examiner. It is my own opinion, that truly great minds are pretty near as immutable, as the great *mind* of all. A conſiſtency of character and behaviour, is the natural reſult of ſuch immutability. Pride, puncto, and a ſenſe of honour, will produce it in certain men; but in thoſe of elevated ſpirits, it is a native principle. Yet, ſuppoſing you to be as frail as malice could wiſh to find, or envy repreſent you; I would be glad to aſk any of the haſty railers at the laſt ſtep you have taken, whether there is the leaſt ſemblance of probability, that any perſon, even of an inferior underſtanding to your own, after being raiſed to ſuch an exalted

pitch

pitch in the eftimaticn of the people, fhould become at once, a kind of political fuicide ; and eclipfe, himfelf, of that glory and luftre, which he was confcious that nothing elfe could overfhadow. I can, however, no longer dwell upon the charge of a demerit in you, grounded on- ly on furmife and inuendo ; perceiving rather an additional impatience in me, to enter upon the more pleafing fubject of your merits, which will neither admit of doubt or contradiction. I fhall not trouble you, good Sir, with many words ; be- caufe your modefty will make you better pleafed with few. Befides, *pauca, fed arguté,* is a leffon I would recommend to the obfervance of all fcribblers. The firft part of the precept, we may with eafe conform to ; I fear the latter is above me.

Al-

Although a merit that fpeaks for itfelf, feems to require no other advocate or voucher ; yet your friends at leaft, may not be difpleafed, with the fhort comparifon I am about to make, between the prefent ftate of the war, and the inglorious circumftances attending the commencement of it.

The French, as you know, Sir, having committed a moft outrageous trefpafs upon the frontiers of *Nova Scotia* ; a proper reprefentation was made of it to our minifters : who, as I have been told, refented it moft highly, and immediately fent over very fpirited remonftrances to the court of *France*, for fo open and unexpected a violation of a treaty, but newly made with them. Happily for us,

their

their difpatches proved fruitlefs and ineffec-
tual. I fay happily, becaufe it fhews,
that their counfels have been as weakly
directed as their arms. For, if they had
had the dexterity and forefight of the *Spa-
niards*, in the year thirty-nine; (who, by
the by, may be doing the fame thing
now) they would not only have difavowed
their governor in his proceedings, and
pleaded ignorance of them; but offered,
as an evidence of their fincerity, to have
recalled, and punifhed him.

By this diffimulation, they had gained
time fufficient, not barely to put themfelves into a pofture of defence, but to
have got together fuch a force in thofe
parts as our utmoft efforts would not have
enabled us to refift. Befides, the affailant,

in

in such cases, having ever an advan-
tage over his enemy, from the secret
consciousness of those designs, whereof the
other can seldom be aware ; the providing of the country with every thing ne-
cessary to make it a place of arms, would
not have been the only use made of such
an interval. For during the suspension of
their intended rupture, no arts had been
unpractised, no means had been left un-
tried, towards extending their interest and
influence amongst the *Indians*. These had
been very important points gained : and
as we know by experience, that a *French*
council is not above such an insidious piece
of policy, it has really surprized me, that
the policy should be above the council.

C   I

I never read *Pere Charlevoix* myfelf; but
have been told by one who has, that in
fome treatife of his, upon the fubject in
queftion, that reverend author had let
flip from his pen an unwary truth: by
afferting, as I am informed, " that the
" interefts of *France* and *England*, in
" *North America*, were utterly incom-
" patible." Such a declaration was
alone fufficient to alarm this country : as
it demonftrated, that, fooner or later, we
were neceffarily to expect, that arduous
conteft between the two nations, for fole
dominion there, in which, I thank hea-
ven and you, we have made fo glorious a
figure. I am juft difcerning enough to
know, Sir, that things great in themfelves, require no aggrandizing : and this
reafoning, forbids me alike, either to
magnify

magnify the conqueft, or to flatter you:
but the entire reduction of that vaft em-
pire, (for fo it may be called) is a moft
ftupendous atchievement.

I fhall take this occafion, as the moft
proper, to affure you, moft folemnly to
affure you, that whatever may fall from
my pen, of the encomiaftic kind, will
be as ingenuous as your own upright
heart. As I have never been the flave of
any man, I have not condefcended either
to be the flatterer of any man; which
is a fpecies of creature *below* a flave:
becaufe a flatterer is a felf-created rep-
tile.————I fhall now purfue my
ftory.

The

The court of *France*, as I had obferved, having excited at once our jealoufy
and indignation, by a moft audacious in-
fraction of their very laft treaty of peace
with us; their inattention to the expediency of retrieving fo unadvifed a ftep, by
all the moft fpecious blinds and fallacies
they could invent; I will take upon me to
fay again, was a moft fortunate event:
the iffue of our quarrel has proved it fo:
for had the contention been referved for a
work of future times, I fcarce perceive a
poffibility, that the vanquifhed could then
have failed of being the conquerors. Yet
our own court, inftead of availing themfelves of this overfight, by an immediate
declaration of war, allowed them ample
time both to fee and rectify their miftake.
We had, it is true, juft refolution enough

to

to make fome reprifals on the enemy; but then all the fhips we took, for want of a more formal annunciation of hoftilities, were reprefented as fo many acts of piracy: and the honour of the nation was fo far from being vindicated by this meafure, that it became daily expofed to frefh impeachments. It is *Tacitus*, I think, who fays, " that certain war is preferable to " uncertain peace, as being a ftate of " greater fecurity* :" but our minifters were not of that opinion. A defcent however, being actually made upon the ifland of *Minorca*, this matter grew a little more ferious; and war was at laft declared, with all the pomp and parade ufually attending fuch ceremonies. Admiral *Byng* was appointed to the command of

the

* Securius Bellum, pace dubiâ.

the fquadron going to its relief; and no-
body had the leaft doubt, (except himfelf) but we fhould make our enemies re-
pent of their hazardous enterprize. The
fequel, alas! is too horrid for remembrance; and as the fhorteft will be the beft
account, for all true lovers of their country,
of his ignominious behaviour, it may
fuffice, to tell them, that the place was
loft in confequence of it. And yet, when
I feem to impute the lofs of *Port Mahon*,
entirely to this unfortunate gentleman, I
ought to explain myfelf: becaufe, in fact,
he was but an acceffary to it. The difap-
pearance of the fleet, and Colonel *Jeffreys*'s
being furprized and taken prifoner, had
a little alarmed and difmayed the garrifon; but the military people then faid,
and ftill fay, that thefe were no reafons

for

for so hasty a surrender of it. Why such honours were heaped upon the governor when he came home, is a secret beyond the reach of my shallow penetration: and yet I will do him the justice to say, that a worthier gentleman never wore them. The conjecture that strikes me most, and therefore satisfies me best, is, that our rulers, in order to avoid the reproach of leaving so important a trust in the hands of an infirm and aged person, obtained for him these extraordinary marks of his majesty's favour, as a proof, not only of their entire approbation of his conduct, but of their conviction, that a younger and more active commander could not have done better. But the real truth is, if they would confess, and a virtual confession of

it

it there was *, that this very confiderable poffeffion of ours, had, unhappily, employed the thoughts and attention of none but our enemies. For, admitting that we had not the means of providing for its outward defence, from a want of fhips fufficient for that purpofe ; yet the fmalleft addition of internal ftrength given to it, by reinforcing of the garrifon, would have obliged the enemy to raife the fiege ; and we had triumphed inftead of the affailants. If what I am faying, feems to caft the leaft reflection upon any man, the perfon fo affected, is to thank himfelf for his mortification. He will find, that the defect was in the object ; for there is no foulnefs in his mirror. *Fari ut poffit quæ fentiat*, is a right that every man of
fpirit,

* The refignation of feveral great employments.

fpirit, will not only affert, but exercife. I
have a very unfeigned love and regard for
certain gentlemen concerned in the admi-
niftration at that time : and if *Palineurus*
fell afleep, there were thofe about him,
who ought to have waked him. It is my
firm opinion, that an abler, better, or
more experienced man, has very rarely
filled his office.————

I have already premifed, good Sir, that
my little animadverfions upon thefe matters, were not, could not be intended, for
the information of a perfon fo capable as
yourfelf, of making more ufeful and judi-
cious reflections upon them. What I had
to fay of yourfelf, I thought would not be
the worfe received, for being faid *to* you.
For the reft, I am only taking the free-

D   dom,

dom, to make you a kind of middle man
between me and the public ; for the information of whom, I have undertaken
this irkfome, and, it may be, thanklefs
tafk.

Not very long ago, being unwarily
drawn into a new difpute, in relation to
the difgrace we had fuffered in the *Mediterranean*, and the dire confequences of it;
a difagreeable incident happened to me in
the debate, a bare recollection whereof,
urges me to enlarge a little upon it : and
although Mr. *Byng*'s fubject cannot but be
hideous from the nature, and tedious from
the tritenefs of it ; you will pardon me,
I dare fay, for recurring to the detefted to-
pic. Amongft other things, I faid I had
been told, that a certain great perfonage,
who

who is now no more, had called him a poltroon, without hearing, or defiring to hear, any other proof of his mifbehaviour, than his own letter. His name being afterwards mentioned, not contemptuoufly, but irreverently enough to give me offence; I fhall bring together fuch a deal of prefumptive evidence, in fupport of the validity of his charge, as may prevent, for the future, any body's telling me, that it was *unwarrantable.*

This gentleman, you are to know, Sir, commanded a fleet in the *Mediterranean* laft war. His commiffion being doubly fuitable to his temper, it pleafed him doubly. He found the *Mediterranean* extremely like the more fouthern ocean; for it proved a rich, and a *pacific* fea. For

D 2   thefe

thefe reafons, during the whole courfe of
the prefent war, he never once follicited
to be employed, unlefs he could have the
fame ftation. He obtained a promife of it
accordingly, which, to our forrow, as
well as to his own, was fatally fulfilled.
But times and circumftances being altered,
there appeared a correfpondent change
too, in the mind · of the Admiral. He
had no fooner got on board, but he began
to make woeful complaints and lamentati-
ons, that he was going to be *facrificed*.
When this apprehenfion was removed, or
rather, obviated, by affurances given him,
that he would be at leaft as ftrong as the
enemy ; he had recourfe to other objecti-
ons, by arraigning Lord *Anfon*, for fend-
ing him out with the worft men in the
whole navy ; and this, before he could
poffibly

poffibly have examined them. The extraordinary time he took, for providing the
fhips with water, at *Gibraltar*, gave room
to fufpect, that part of it might be fpent
in making his own *. But the more pro-
bable reafon, to fpeak ferioufly, was, that
he hoped, by this delay, to give the *French*
Admiral fo many more chances to hear of
his approach : in confequence of which,
he was not without fome expectation, that
he would try to avoid him by a retreat.

We are come now to the defperate en-
gagement, in which our tongue-doughty
commander, as well as his friends, declared that he had beaten the adverfe fleet ;
though

---

* The gentlemen of the navy tell me, that the
firft impreffions of fear among the common failors,
fhew themfelves by profufe evacuations of this fort.

though he had notorioufly left them in poffeffion of all they wanted; which was covering the fiege of *Philipfburgh*. But notwithftanding our unfortunate chief was fo wary in fight, he was very unwary in counfel : for he contradicted himfelf the next day. By which we have reafon to apprehend, that his head was not much better than his heart. Having called a council of war upon this occafion, the firft queftion, I believe, that he moved to the board, was, whether, if he returned to the charge, and attacked the enemy again, they thought it would be of any great fer- vice ? It was decided in the negative. But it may not be improper to obferve in this place, that a routed or fhattered fleet, feldom remains in the way of being beaten a fecond time. Another query which Mr.

Prefident

Prefident put to the council, was, whether a total defeat of the *French* fquadron,
could be any ways conducive to the faving
of *Port Mahon* ? And it was agreed that
it certainly would not. But the fallacy of
this argument, is too glaring to pafs un-
noticed : for the fame reafon would have
held good, for not attacking Mr. Galiffi-
onere, if he had met him in the channel.
Our Admiral, I confefs, was univerfally
reputed a good mariner ; but fuch a tefti-
monial gives no idea at all, of his qualifications for a commander. Though fea-
manfhip might be of ufe to him in direct-
ing his fhip, it no ways enables a man to
direct himfelf. But if we fhould difcover,
that this very able feaman, had acted
moft notorioufly unlike a feaman ; it will
befpeak no want of candour, to conclude

he

he had his private reason for it. Now, the renowned Mr. *Boscawen*, Sir, on being properly informed of the disposition made by Admiral *Byng* that day, and his approaches to the enemy; and being asked whether he approved of it; very modestly made answer, that he *believed* he should have formed his attack in another manner. I think I can pretty perfectly relate what he said, though I do not perfectly understand it. He should have chosen, he said, to have gone up in a line of battle a-head, to some appointed distance, from which he would have given his Captains orders to depart, like a file of musqueteers : by which means, all his own ships had been equi-distant from those they were respectively to oppose, on the side of the enemy.

But

But this would not have ferved our he-
ro's purpofe. His bufinefs was to come
within the letter of fighting, and not
within the letter of cowardice. And
although I am no feaman, I think, I may
venture to pronounce, that he never, in
all his life, trimmed, or fteered a veffel,
to fo critical a nicety.

Though I fhall, probably, never be in
the way of hearing your fentiments of this
well meant addrefs to you ; yet I fhall
flatter myfelf with the fecret perfuafion,
of having given you a moft thorough conviction, that there were fome fymptoms
at leaft, of pufillanimity about this man.
But the firft perfon in the kingdom, (who
was, of courfe, the moft immediately
and fenfibly affected by his mifdemeanour)

E   having

having been blamed for giving a preju-
dicate opinion upon the cafe ; I fhall certainly be very cautious of faying, that Mr.
Byng acted like a coward ; but I will for
ever fay, and infift upon it, that a coward
would have acted like Mr. *Byng*. And
yet, the very beft evidence of all remains
ftill behind. For many of the feamen,
who were allowed to go afhore at *Gibraltar*, in order to refrefh themfelves ; as
foon as ever they underftood, that this fla-
gitious tranfaction had been taken cogni-
zance of at home, and the Admiral was
to be put under arreft, made no fcruple to
infult him in the ftreet ; by afking him,
in derifion, " why he did not go, and
" bury his dead." Which humourous
piece of irony, feems ftrongly to denote,
that he had taken all due care, not to be

in

in the bills of mortality, upon fo trivial an occafion.

This relation, I fear, may have been fomewhat tedious : but the perfon who is the fubject of it, (though a moft execrable actor) having had fo confiderable a part, in the tragical fcene I am exhibiting; it feemed fufficiently to coincide with my general defign, not to be thought wholly impertinent. Befides, I have reafon to think, that I cannot but have told the reader fome few things, which perfons, lefs inquifitive and follicitous than myfelf, about all national concerns, could not have told him. If the wrath I perceive in myfelf againft the poor man, had been kindled in me by any other caufe, than his not being a man, I could with eafe

E 2   have

have curbed it. But he that has publicly suffered death, for having betrayed the interests of his King and Country, may very fairly be regarded, as a personal enemy, of all true lovers of them. That character I have assumed, and would invariably adhere to it, at any hazard. A luke-warm patriot, like a luke-warm friend, may make parade and boast of his affection ; but its efficiency, in point of services, I doubt, would not be great. Though the present times do not appear the aptest for such a confession, I will own to you, Sir, that I have a little tincture of enthusiasm in my composition : and, urged by the irresistible influence of it, I have indulged my resentment of Mr. *Byng*'s offence, with great scope : yet not from any hatred I bore to him, but from an abhorrence of his crime.

crime. Nor had I, perhaps, disturbed
the ashes of the dead at all, but with a
view, and hope, of giving consolation
to the living: by which I mean, those
few of his judges, who, from misconceived
sentiments of humanity, had felt a
little compunction about the sentence past
upon him. Had I the pleasure to be better
known to those gentlemen, they would
know too, that there is not a man on earth,
of a less fierce or sanguinary disposition than
myself : yet I take this occasion to aver,
that had I been one of them, I could have
condemned him, not only without scruple,
but without regret. Nay more ; my enmity
would have followed him, even to
the grave. Mr. *Addison*, I remember,
puts a most heroic ejaculation into the
mouth of his *Cato*, when he is surveying
the

the body of his flaughtered fon, by making him fay, " what pity 'tis, that we can " die but once to ferve our country ? " Whether fuch a fentiment is not a little too refined, to be the fuggeftion of nature, I fhall not take upon me to decide : but it is really a pity, in my opinion, that a man can die but once, for difterving his country.

After having clofed my evidence, and apologized for protracting it into fo great a length ; the afking leave to fubjoin one other circumftance, may fomewhat furprize you. It is not at all relative to the Admiral's crime, but to his character, very much fo : becaufe it will difcover in him, a thorough depravity of heart. As you fat many years in parliament with

this

this gentleman, where you have feen him daily paffing and repaffing through the houfe; I am perfuaded, he did not efcape your notice. And if your infight into men, be only half as quick as your penetration into other matters; you could not but obferve, that nature herfelf feemed to have marked him, for all unnatural things.

The circumftance at which I have already hinted, and am about to tell you, is, that when Admiral *Matthews* was tried for fome irregularities in his conduct, whilft he commanded in the *Mediterranean*, Mr. *Byng* was prefident of the court-martial; and this blood-thirfty warriour, whom we have proved to be cautious at leaft of fhedding his own, when he came to fum up the evidence, and make report of it, departed

parted from the accuſtomed form and me-
thod of ſuch tribunals, of aſking firſt,
ſeriatim, the ſentiments of the other judges
upon it, by prematurely declaring it to be
his opinion, " that Mr. *Matthews*'s of-
" fences were capital, and he ought to ſuf-
" fer death." I think that the warmeſt of
Mr. *Byng*'s friends will not offer to exte-
nuate ſo enormous a proceeding.

The doctrine of Providence, Sir, I mean
a ſpecial Providence, in the direction of
human affairs, is attended with ſo much
doubt and perplexity; I am not become
ſufficiently maſter of this point of religi-
ous faith, to be able to ſay, that I have
attributed a great deal to it. But were I
a more firm believer of the hypotheſis, I
could with very little difficulty be per-
ſuaded,

suaded, that the fate to which this infatuated wretch had at last exposed himself, was an operation of the divine will, in the way of retribution, for the cruel wrong he had attempted to do that gallant officer. When I call him so, I speak with authority; for Sir *Charles Wager*, in characterising him, expressed himself figuratively upon the occasion : by saying, " that he was stout, but when he came into " action, he was not sure, that he had quite " ballast enough in him:" meaning, by this metaphor, to intimate, that his courage was unquestionable, though he had not altogether the same alliance in his conduct.

Too conscious, Sir, of my tedious detention of you in the *Mediterranean*, a sea so unpropitious to our arms; I shall carry

F

you

you a long voyage, in a very short time, by
transporting you at once to *North America*;
where our miscarriages were not less
alarming or disgraceful, though, ultimately, not so fatal. Of the gentlemen
employed upon that service, we were most
beholden to those who were most inactive:
they that did the least, did the best : yet
the *vis inertiæ*, is certainly not a force,
calculated for making conquests. I wish
that Mr. *Braddock* had been a better General, though I had been so much worse
a prophet : for I foretold, that if he met
with any difficulty, he would indubitably
be foiled and brought to shame. 'Twas
thought, that he had never considered his
calling as a matter of art and science, in
all his life. He was extremely superficial,
and yet proud, opinionative, and overbear-
ing :

ing : had never liked his profeffion, nor did any of his profeffion like him. This laft article of his difqualification, for the very important truft repofed in him, de-ferved, alone, a little more attention, than feemed to have been paid it : for I pre-fume, a thorough confidence in its leader, is the very life and foul of an army. Sup-pofing a General to be a thorough able man, I confefs, indeed, that the fenfible part of the officers who are to ferve under him, may, without efteeming him, have that implicit reli ance on his conduct, fo apparently requifite, to promote the fer-vice. But this is not the cafe of the com-mon foldier, who is to be governed by his affections, and not his reafon. The heart of fuch a wretch, will ever be beft recon-ciled to his defperate work, when the

com-

commander is in poffeffion of it. Talking
of Mr. *Braddock* one day to a gentleman,
who, during his fhort command in the
Eaft Indies, did himfelf fo much honour
there; he could not help faying, that I
feemed to have known him very tho-
roughly. The expofing his army to be furprized and baffled by a fmall detachment
of the enemy's, confifting chiefly of *Indians,* was owing, 'tis faid, to his obftinate
refufal to take with him any irregulars of
that fort; though it was generally thought,
that they would have been of the utmoft
ufe to him, by fkirting his troops during
their march, and keeping off an enemy,
that, as he had managed matters, gave
them great annoyance, and, almoft, without making themfelves vifible*.   But his
conduct

* This happened in paffing the river *Ohio.*

conduct fubfequent to the confternation, which he faw the whole army thrown into, examined by the teft of common fenfe, feemed very prepofterous. What could be expected of poor creatures, agitated by a terror, fo naturally fcattered among them, from beholding, at one time, an officer falling before them, and, at another, their right or left hand man ? and to quicken their refentment of this horrid flaughter, it was made by an enemy, on whom there was not a poffibility of their making any reprifals. For thefe reafons; As foon as ever the General had tried all means of forming, or getting them forwards, and faw the impracticability of either, the advifable part next, was, furely, to get them back again: and, as he could not remove the panic, to re-

move

move the men. I have been told, not-
withstanding, that some hours had past,
before he was sensible of the expediency of
making his retreat.——Being an exceed-
ing gallant man, I wish most sincerely,
that he had survived this unfortunate en-
counter; for he had spent the greatest
part of his life, in very distressful circumstances; and pretty soon after they
were become more easy, he lost it. I
know not how true it is, but I have been
told, that when he was made Captain General of all his Majesty's forces in *North-
America,* he never before had had the
command of five hundred men, upon any
occasion whatever. A Colonel's com-
mission, is not to be admitted as a disproof
of this assertion; because a man's being at
the

the head of a regiment at home, is no executive command, moſt undoubtedly.

War, and the calamitous conſequences of it, making a part of thoſe unavoidable evils, to which the human paſſions have ſubjeᴄted ſocieties; and the iſſue and deciſions of it, being of the utmoſt importance to us : how peculiarly cautious ought our miniſters to be, in the choice of thoſe perſons, with whom they intruſt the care and conduᴄt of our military operations. And I am of opinion, that the knowledge of men's charaᴄters and abilities, with a proper direᴄtion of our enquiries, is not ſo difficult to come at, as is generally thought. And yet, you want not to be told, my good Sir, that in another inſtance, beſide the preſent, we ſuffered a moſt igno

minious

minious defeat, where we ought to have obtained a compleat victory. ✳

By the foregoing account, Sir, I seem to have but shifted the scene, without changing my reprefentation. The fatality that had attended our mifdoings in the other hemifphere, appeared to have made alliance with us, and accompanied our forces to *America*. We had been before difpoffeffed of our ftrength at *Ofwego*, and now failed of the reprifal we hoped to make, by an attempt upon *Fort du Quefne*. What I am relating, is from my memory only, and that a bad one ; but I think the other divifions of our army, though conducted by gentlemen of fufficient fkill and prowefs, through the infinite difficulties and obftacles, neceffarily attending

all

✳ At Ticonderoga

all military operations in fuch a country, had done little or nothing. Under the noble Lord who was next appointed to the command of the forces, and allowed to be very capable; our army, to the beft of my remembrance, made no movement at all. That, and every thing elfe, for I know not how long, remained in a ftate of utter inaction.

His Lordfhip, however, having at laft received his Majefty's orders, to make a defcent at *Cape Breton*, and to take with him fuch a part of the troops, as he fhould think fufficient for the enterprize; as foon as the tranfports could be got ready, he fet out upon this important expedition. But the General thinking it advifable to have the opinions of a council of war, (which

G   fcarce

scarce ever fail to end in counsels of peace)
an assembly of this sort was accordingly
convened, in order to deliberate upon his
Majesty's instructions. And the result of
the consultation, in effect, was; that
the sense of his council at home, was not
the sense of his council abroad; for they
were unanimously of opinion, that the lay-
ing siege to *Louisburg*, was too hazardous
an undertaking, to be attempted with any
good effect to the service. His Lordship,
in consequence of this resolution, aban-
doned the enterprize, and returned to the
place from whence he came. This cruel
disappointment, however, of the good
King's, as well as the nation's hopes,
helped to verify the paradoxical position
I set out with; which was, that we never
did so well for ourselves, as when we were
doing

doing nothing. For, during this fruitlefs, but not expencelefs expedition, the enemy availed themfelves of our General's abfence, and took fort *William Henry*, upon the lake *George*; which could not otherwife have been loft. General *Webb*, not having received the fuccours he expected from the colonies, could not afford to fend any to the neighbouring garrifon : apprehending, that the force he had with him, was barely fufficient for the fecurity of fort *Edward* : which was the only barrier, or place of defence remaining, to prevent the enemy's immediate entrance into *Albany*.

——If you have thought it worth your while, Sir, to attend to this mortifying relation, from beginning to end ; a remark I have made upon it to myfelf, may, poffibly, have occurred to you : which is,

G 2

that we made war, before we declared it, and, as foon as we had declared it, ceafed to make it.

Into this helplefs, hopelefs, and groveling ftate were we funk, when the good genius of the nation called you forth, to attend and affift its councils : and feemed to tell us, that the *revocare gradum*, was a tafk and honour referved for Mr. *Pitt*. You took upon you the *Herculean* labour, and have performed it in a manner, that has aftonifhed all the world. I am aware, that I have expreffed myfelf upon this occafion, in an uncommon way : yet not from any affectation of figurative and pompous phrafe ; but from thinking you a very uncommon man. I might, from my own breaft derive one proof, that you cannot

cannot but have fome great peculiarities belonging to you; becaufe I both love and envy you extremely : which are affections, that few have ever reconciled.

Having taken notice, in general terms, of the wondrous fuccefs of our arms, under your aufpicious guidance of them : to enumerate the particular conquefts, and acquifitions, would, doubtlefs, be thought a work of fupererogation. The children in the ftreets, can recount our glorious fpoils; and their children's children will revere you for them. I fhall, therefore, turn my thoughts, at prefent, to the horrideft fubject that ever employed them : I mean the very unnatural and ungrateful requital you have met with. I do not fcruple to aver, abftractedly from the partiality I may

have

have towards you, that any attempt to traduce a character and fame like yours, appears to me a crime, not greatly inferiour to blafphemy: efpecially, as the offender would be guilty only of a foolifh piece of impiety, in one inftance; and might do an irreparable injury in the other. But cenfure, fays the famous Doctor *Swift*, is a tax which all merit pays to the publick: and if this, like moft other affeffments, is proportioned to what we poffefs, you are not to wonder, Sir, that you have been fo highly rated. I acknowledge myfelf, notwithftanding, to be lefs difagreecbly affected, by the perfonal injury done to you, than by the dreadful apprehenfion I have conceived, of the mifchievous tendency, to the whole, of that fpirit of envy, fo very

rife

rife amongſt us, that it is almoſt become
an univerſal paſſion. Poor virtue, is already in ſuch a languid and declining ſtate,
that ſhe wants every cordial and provoca-
tive that can poſſibly be adminiſtered, if
we wiſh her to recover : ſhe has not the
leaſt chanee to live, if we ſuffer her to
be brought lower. Now, fame, my good Sir,
being the prime incentive to great and virtuous deeds; whatever is ſaid, or done, towards
leſſening the object, in the mind of its
purſuer, has a tendency to deprive the
publick, of the advantages ariſing to our-
ſelves, from ſo laudable an ambition. For
they that, animated by your example,
might hereafter have become candidates
for this noble prize ; upon finding it of ſo
precarious a tenure, would be apt to think
the lubricious poſſeſſion, no longer worthy,

thy, either of their care, or emulation.
when this fhall come to be the cafe, the
authors of fo lamentable a cataftrophe, may
fairly be called traytors to the community.
The treatment you yourfelf have lately
met with, has led me to imagine, that
our proverbial maxim, which holds virtue
to be its own reward ; was originally
grounded upon the obfervation, that it
feldom meets with any other. And as
your experience is verifying my comment
upon this adage ; I hope, and truft,
that your own thoughts are miniftering to
you, the comfort promifed in the text.

In fearching after the fource of this
fatal evil, it appeared to me to be wholly
owing to the prenicious error we are in,
of making dull and low-minded men learned.

ed. Blinded by a vain prepoffeffion in favour of our own offspring, every mechanic
thinks, that a Mercury may be made of
his block, as well as another's. The poor
boy, *invitâ Naturâ*, is accordingly fent
to fome great fchool : and the Peda-
gogue, under whom he has paft his ini-
tiation, having rough-hewn the image,
the deluded parent perfifts in his folly,
and fends his idol to be finifhed at the
univerfity. When he returns from thence,
what is to become of this mifguided
creature! Why, inftead of the chiffel,
his natural inheritance from the induftri-
ous father, he betakes himfelf to his pen;
but not having the talents requifite to
make it either ufeful or entertaining, how
to employ this unwieldly weapon, is the
point that puzzles him. Urged, at laft,

H   by

by the little knowledge he has of human
nature, and the depravity of his own, his
thoughts and labors are turned entirely to
abufe. Writing, Sir, in this country, is
become altogether as much a trade, as
any handicraft occupation whatever.
And every dealer in this dirty traffic, too
foon apprifed of the tafte of the times,
and the certainty of finding in his cuf-
tomers, a competent portion of the fame
curfed paffion, which prompted himfelf
to his iniquitous work ; utters his poi-
fonous and infectious folly to his credu-
lous readers, with fuch unbounded licence,
that nothing good, refpectable, or facred
amongft men, is fuffered to live, becaufe
they muft.

One

One of thefe mercenary railers at you, was gotten fo very low in the expreffions of his malice, that, upon my veracity, I did not underftand the terms he ufed ; he faid you deferved a *fhell*. After repeated enquiries about the fignification of the word, I was informed at laft, that it was a piece of cant at the gallows, when the . friends of the perfon to be executed, had provided a *coffin* for him. Judge, my good Sir, whether I have not reprefented thefe pefts of fociety very properly : when we can no longer read their fcurrilous jargon, without the help of a gloffary from St. *Giles*'s.———After what I have faid, concerning thefe inferiour drudges of the Printers ; I am forry to tell you, that I have been acquainted with one or two

H 2   very

very upright, truly knowing, and able perfonages, who, from the like contracted circumstances, have been under the same predicament. And as I have always been a most unfeigned friend and admirer, of learned and ingenious men; had a state of affluence ever been my lot, the professions I am now making of my good will towards them, were entirely needless : for, if I know myself at all, they would have found in me, a pretty confiderable patron.

I am not enough acquainted with your formation and temperament, to be able to judge at all, what impreffion these brutal violences may have made upon you. But left you should be affected by them, beyond what they deferve ; I beg leave

to

to prefcribe for you, an antidote to all heart-burnings fo created. This famous recipe, Sir, directs you, to mix with your indignation, a double portion of contempt : which will fo qualify and moderate your refentment of moft things, as to make them very fupportable. I am too fcrupulous, to recommend to you a medicine I had not tried; but I have very lately had occafion to make ufe of this, and can affure you, that it moft effectually anfwered my purpofe.

If my experience had not long ago taught me, to wonder at nothing ; how the viciffitudes in your fortune would have furprized me. The *ventofa plebs* are moft happily defcribed, by the celebrated poet who makes ufe of that expreffion,

preſſion, in one ſingle epithet : becauſe
they literally veer to and fro, like the
winds themſelves. They that, but a
month ago, thought your character the
moſt emaculate in the world; now fancy
on a ſudden, that they have diſcovered as
many flaws and ſpots in it, as are to be
found in an emblem of *bad fame :* whereas, if there were really any blemiſhes in
it, they ought to have been regarded but
like the ſpots in the ſun ; which are
barely left viſible, by the great aſcendant
the brighter parts of it's body have over
them. I have been told, that ſome of the
venal, virulent crew I have been menti-
oning, have made it matter of wonder,
that you ſhould ever aſpire at being a mi-
niſter in a country like this ; where pro-
perty has ſuch an abſolute influence over

all

all things : alledging very emphatically, that you are not even a landed man ! I moſt heartily lament the truth they tell me, yet cannot but hope their inference is falſe. For if theſe terreſtrial qualifications, are to have a preference to the moſt diſtinguiſhed ſpiritual powers, in the choice of miniſters ; what is to become of us ! Are you not apprehenſive, Sir, when we come to be governed by gentlemen of this deſcription only, that we ſhall find moſt of our acre-wiſe rulers, to be no better than wiſe-acres ? The danger to me appears very imminent. But the advancing of this abſurd propoſition, while the dominion Sir *Robert Walpole* had acquired in this country, is ſo freſh in our memories, makes the ſolæciſm more glaring : for I believe it is pretty notorious,

rious, that his eftate, originally, did not greatly exceed, the qualification requifite for a Knight of a fhire.

You have probably obferved, Sir, tho' I have occafionally rebuked, the impotent malice of the *fcabies* of your flanderers, that I have not yet touched upon the fubject of your more confiderable accufers. My reafon for it is, that when the allegations of fuch cenfors fhall come in queftion, I intend, as well as I am able, to give anfwers to them all. In the mean time, I hope that neither the fpite of one, or the falfe reafonings and fufpicions of the other, will give you a moment's difquiet. Your character is above the reach, your fpirit fhould fet you above the regard of both. Your fame is fo

efta-

eftablifhed, that you may defy the moft malicious of its affailants. Though they come armed with the panoply of falfehood and envy, thofe inveterate enemies of all diftinguifhed merit, they will find their arrows recoil, and that the object is invulnerable. I am perfuaded at leaft, that your refentment of the outrageous indignities that have been put upon you, will neither abate of your zeal and follicitude for the public fervice, or produce the leaft change in any part of your future conduct. Men of enlarged and liberal minds, can reft fatisfied with the confcioufnefs of having done praife-worthy actions ; the praife itfelf is but a fecondary confideration, and therefore of lefs account with them. The noble fentiment Lord *Sommers*

I

bore

bore about his efcutcheon *, you bear about your heart : and though your fervices have neceffarily made you fo confpicuous, your firft ambition, I dare fay, was to render yourfelf ufeful to fociety.

Perceiving myfelf, notwithftanding the fecret pleafure that has accompanied my labour, to grow a little weary of this friendly office ; I begin to fear, that your perufal of it will not be unattended, with fome fimilar fenfations. For this reafon, I fhall detain you no longer now, than will be neceffary to fulfil my promife, and finally releafe you.

The firft article of the ill fupported charge brought againft you, is, that your meafures,

---

* Prodeffe quam confpici.

meafures, fince you was in power, have not been conformable to your doctrines and opinions, when you was out of power. This allegation feems to imply, that although a fecond confideration of things is thought fo advifable, as to be proverbially recommended to our practice ; you are never to change *your* opinion, under the moft thorough conviction, that you have been in an error. The inference I draw from this, to fhew myfelf as good a logician as my adverfary, is, that what daily experience makes venial in one man, was not allowable in another. Within thefe few years, an act * paffed in one feffion of parliament, was repealed in the enfuing one : and yet I never heard, that the worthy gentleman, who thought fit to make this fudden alteration in his meafures, in-

curred

* The naturalization of the *Jews*.

curred the leaft cenfure or reproach, in confequence of his inconfiftency. Second thoughts, however, in that inftance, did but remedy, what a previous ufe of them might have prevented. Neverthelefs, I do not mean to reft your caufe upon the authority of an example or two ; I can produce irrefragable reafons, in behalf of your converfion. Practical truths depend fo much upon circumftances that we are to vary our conduct, according to the variations of them. To be able to fay what ought to be, we fhould firft know what is : and without intuitive powers, how could you be this entire mafter of his Majefty's fituation, before you was admitted to a fhare in his counfels ? Befides, if every thing defirable were immediately attainable, whence arifes the tedious fuf-

penfion

penſion of our much longed for peaee !
But I ſhall endeavour to recollect the ſub-
ſtance of part of a ſpeech you made about
three years ago, when the continuation of
the war in *Germany* came in queſtion. Not
being in the houſe myſelf, you will be
pleaſed, Sir, to make allowance, for the
deceptions to which I am liable, both
from the failure of my memory, and the
miſleadings of my informer. One of your
arguments, if I remember right, contained
the moſt obvious and undeniable piece of
good ſenſe conceiveable : which was, that if
we kept any troops there at all, it was ad-
viſable to ſend more ; in order to effectu-
ate the intended ſervice of your meaſure :
which, uneffected, would be attended
with a diſſervice of the moſt inhuman
kind. You reaſoned nobly, my good Sir ;
and

and nothing could be wanting, but a little fellow-feeling, to make every man in the kingdom think like yourfelf. For to fuffer fuch brave creatures, to oppofe themfelves to an enemy, outnumbering them in the proportion of three to one, would have been a cruelty little inferior to a maffacre. If I miftake not, you pleaded farther in vindication of yourfelf, that it was not then a time to tell your private thoughts of what *had* been done; but to conduct yourfelf fuitably to the circumftances in which you found yourfelf, and make the beft of them : that there was a concatenation of things, in refpect of ftate matters, that did not always admit of being feparately confidered; for as much as the leaft breach in fuch a chain, might entirely difconcert the whole plan. If you will allow me,

Sir,

Sir, to make a fhort fupplement, to this
very well followed argumentation; I fhould
add, that, as your own fovereign had
brought himfelf into very diftrefsful circumftances, by afferting the rights and li-
berties of his *Englifh* fubjects; and his
great kinfman, in confequence of his
alliance with him, into much worfe;
the fituation of both feemed very com-
miferable; and not only to deferve, but
claim, the confideration of this country.
But left I fhould be mifconceived, upon
the fubject of this unpopular doctrine;
it may be neceffary fo far to explain myfelf, as to tell the reader, it is *pro hac vice*
only, that I am an advocate for it. I
moft ardently wifh, and not without fome
degree of hope, to fee my good country-
men come unanimoufly to a refolution,

never

never more to be the champions of *Hano-*
ver, or precipitately hurried into conti-
nental wars, upon that antiquated, vifio-
nary notion, of preferving a ballance of
power in *Europe*. The ballance of power
in *Europe*, is not to be maintained, by
any political equation table : it is as fure
to find its level, in time, as any branch of
trade. But not to leave this queftion altogether in a problematic ftate ; you will
permit me to remind you of the *Dutch* war,
in which the weak counfels, of the weak-
eft Prince that ever filled a throne, had
involved his poor infatuated fubjects.
This extraordinary meafure; feems to bring
home the point in debate : becaufe it totally fubverted the ridiculous fyftem we
are talking of. And yet, what was the
iffue of that war ; why our good old *friends*,

emerged

emerged from a ftate, almoft, of annihi-
lation; and obtained pretty near as good a
peace for themfelves, as if they had been
conquerors. We might, neverthelefs, purfue this *ignis fatuus* to a certain length,
provided we did not make fuch vaft facri-
fices to the phantom. But fhould this er-
roneous principle again revive, and, upon
being rendered a little more expedient and
practicable, become again a ftate maxim;
even in that cafe, our manner of proceeding,
fuppofing *England* to be the grand equili-
librift, would prove us fundamentally de-
ficient in our praxis. Becaufe every ba-
lance is brought to it's equability, by the
laft influence given to it : whereas, it has
always been our cuftom to get into the
fcale firft. Add to this, Sir, that, in forming any political fyftem, in fupport whereof,

K   we

we rely upon the affiftance of other powers, deemed reciprocally benefitted by it, we fhall often be deceived. It cannot but happen, that the parties to fuch an affociation, allured, at different times, by views of a more immediate intereft, will renounce their confederacy; the fcheme of the projector, end like that of an alchemift; and the devifer of it find himfelf, the bubble of his own chimera. I think, ere now, that you have anticipated the drift of this little epifode: which has been, ultimately, to remind you, of the main condition of our laft treaty of peace with *France*. By the reftoring of *Cape Breton*, which was all we had got in the laft war, we procured peace and reftitution for both our allies: whofe manner of requiting us, for their fignal

and

and unexpected redemption, is never to be forgotton : *Holland*, in the beginning of the prefent war, having been fomething worfe than neutral ; and the Queen of *Hungary*, immediately meditating and contriving the deftruction of our great confederate. The object you perceive, Sir, under our prefent confideration, was, in this inftance, totally loft fight of; and feemed to have no more real exiftence in it, than the fcales in the *Zodiac:* for the two 'forementioned ftates, were formerly the moft confiderable of our balance-mafters.

——A *query*, whether any thing fo vague and fluctuating, as the point in queftion, be worthy of our further attention, is the natural conclufion of my theorem.——

K 2   I

I am at laft returned, to a fubject much more interefting, though, in itfelf, lefs pleafing: being about to tell you, that your mortal fin, with the *public*, is your having taken a penfion. To which I anfwer, that the principle of felf-denial is a virtue that we may with eafe lay claim to, while we af-fert it only at the expence of others : but it is indubitably the cafe, wherein fpeculation and practice, will always differ moft. And I am as much convinced, as I am of my being, that of all the carping, cavilling multitude, who have condemn'd you for taking this penfion, not a fingle man would have himfelf refufed it. It is far-ther to be obferved, that, on the one hand, not a foul was interefted, in your declining his Majefty's bounteous offer; and, on the other, that nature, honour, and com-

mon

mon prudence, jointly called upon you to ac-
cept it. 'Tis the bufinefs, I fhall not
exprefs myfelf improperly, if I fay it
is the duty of every man, to make the
beft of his being, in his natural capacity;
and the moft of his abilities, in his focial
one. The exertion of your abilities, Sir,
we have fo fenfibly felt, that the whole
nation have expreffed their fenfe of them :
but your virtuous labours being feemingly
at an end ; we are, at prefent, very mo-
deftly and gratefully requiring of you, to
leave yourfelf, the only perfon, unbene-
fitted by them. The urgency of your
provocation to withdraw yourfelf from
council, is fufficiently evinced, by the fa-
crifice you made, to your refentment of
what was doing there, For if, upon
mercenary motives, you refigned an employment

ployment of five or fix thoufand pounds
a-year, for a penfion of three; you may
be a great Statefman, Sir, but you are a
moft forry Arithmetician.

The imputation next attempted to be
fixed upon you, is, that you have been
too abfolute and headftrong: which article of your impeachment, is partly admitted, and in part denied. That you
have *not* been abfolute, we have reafon to
lament; but that you are headftrong, we
allow. Our enemies have felt that
ftrength, the nation has applauded, your
king requited, and only your competitors
for power, decried it.

This relation having been interfperfed
with many marks of my partiality for
you;

you; you will eafily believe, that the
giving you up in any point, cannot fail to
be attended with great mortification to
me. And yet, there is a part of your in-
dictment ftill remaining, to which I could
fay very little for you : I mean, the infup-
portable expences of this war. For if you
had fubdued (as, to be fure, you might
have done) the moft formidable power in
Europe, without the ufe of arms; or
employed thofe arms, without the ufe of
money; your merit towards us, had been,
doubtlefs, much greater, than it is at
prefent.

I was not aware of my overfight 'till this
moment ; but I have greatly mifmanaged
the conduct of my apology for you, in
referving, for the laft, an allegation, to
which,

which, as your attorney, I was obliged to plead guilty. The arrogant intimation you have given the public, of your having had the direction of his Majefty's counfels, for fome time paft, is wholly inexcufable: becaufe, knowing it to be a moft profound fecret; as a cabinet counfellor, you certainly ought not to have difclofed it. Raillery apart, the extravagant futilities I have been peftered with, in the guife of arguments, upon a moft plain and fimple queftion, are fo far from entitling the advancers of them, to be ftiled reafoners; that they are fo many violences done to reafon : which is the effence of all *truth*. And thence, I prefume, it is, that the Deity himfelf, according to the fcriptures, is called *reafon*.

To

To bring this motly narrative to a conclufion; I fhall endeavour to requite my
own labors, with the fecret fatisfaction
of telling myfelf, you cannot but have
obferved, in the courfe of it, that my eyes
have been upon you, for almoft thirty
years paft: and, in confequence of this
obfervation, that you have done me the
juftice likewife to notice, the manifeft
impoffibility of one man's ingroffing the
attention of another fo long, without a
confiderable fhare of his regard. And
to tell you true, I have not only loved you
a great while, but in a peculiar manner.
The capricious likings of perfons of different fexes, are fo very natural, and, befides, fo common ; that where they excite any wonder, the admirer himfelf is

L   to

to be wondered at. But friendfhips, formed by a fympathetic attraction, and, as it were, an intuitive impulfe, are not fo frequent. And yet, it was by fome fecret influence of this fort, that you became at firft poffeffed of my efteem. That this attachment was not wholly void of vanity and felf love, I am ready to confefs : my firft propenfity towards it, having arifen from feeing, or thinking I faw, great refemblance of myfelf in you.

I have, in the opening of this letter, made known, that I had formerly fat in parliament with you ; and am at prefent lamenting, but chiefly upon your account, that I did not, in defpite of my mifufage, keep my feat there. In fuch a fcene of action, you might have had more ample

proofs

proofs of my friendſhip for you : becauſe, " my deeds would have borne witneſs of " me." And though the repeated checks and traverſes of an untoward fortune, had, very long ago, exhauſted my broken and dejected ſpirit ; I ſhould have found ſome means, even in the capacity of one of your mutes, to have occaſionally done you ſome little credit. Animated like-wiſe by your example, that ſpirit of emu-lation, which, in my younger days, I per-ceived ſo active in my boſom, as almoſt to diſquiet it ; might have again taken place there ; and, with a kind of elaſtic force, created by its former preſſures, ſprung with redoubled vigour. Ambition, that inconſiſtent ſource of good and evil, had, even at the Univerſity, taken root in me : And if I was not groſsly flattered there,

few,

few, if any requifites were thought want=
ing in me, for the gratification of it.
Yet, unfortunately, not being my own
mafter; by an arbitrary and perverfe direction of my little talents afterwards, to
a ftudy moft invincibly diftafteful to me;
thofe gifts of nature degenerated into
curfes : and, like Narciffus's beauty, became the ruin of their poffeffor. — But it
is neither fafe, nor feemly, for an afflicted
perfon, to expatiate over much, upon the
fubject of himfelf: I fhall, therefore, no
farther trefpafs on my reader.

Let me conjure you, finally, my good
fir, moft firmly to fuftain your pride : becaufe I am experimentally convinced, that
your pride will help to fuftain *you*. I mean
that virtuous pride, which dwells in every

well

www.ingramcontent.com/pod-product-compliance
Lightning Source LLC
Chambersburg PA
CBHW020333090426
42735CB00009B/1516